# ADD & SUBTRACT

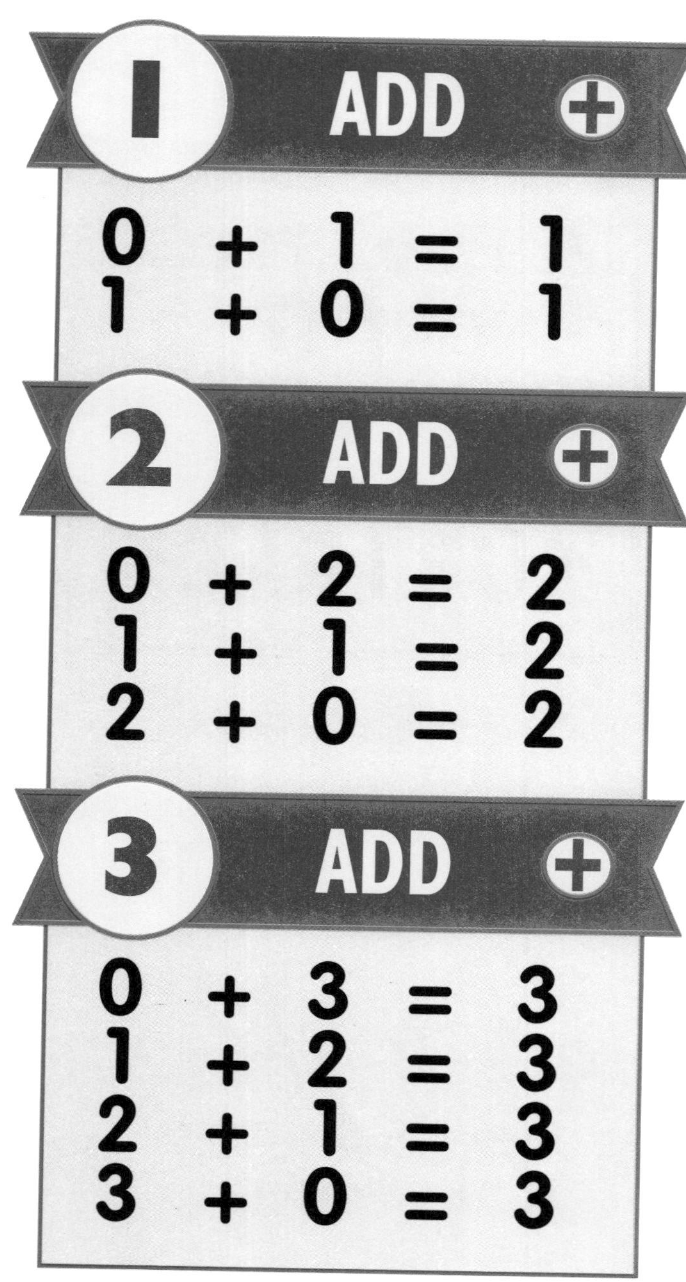
1 ADD +
0 + 1 = 1
1 + 0 = 1
2 ADD +
0 + 2 = 2
1 + 1 = 2
2 + 0 = 2
3 ADD +
0 + 3 = 3
1 + 2 = 3
2 + 1 = 3
3 + 0 = 3

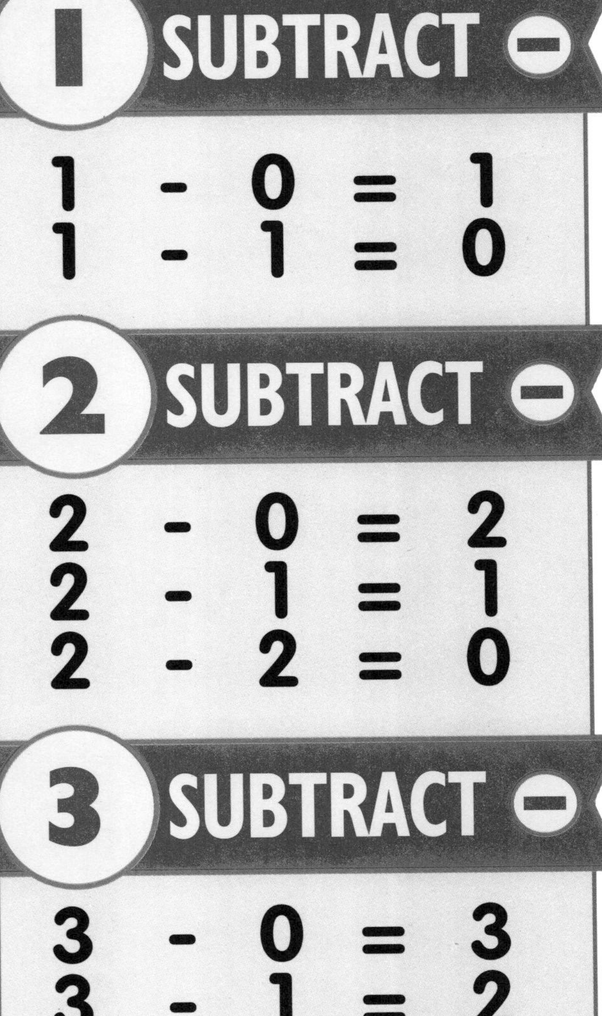

## 1 SUBTRACT −

1 - 0 = 1
1 - 1 = 0

## 2 SUBTRACT −

2 - 0 = 2
2 - 1 = 1
2 - 2 = 0

## 3 SUBTRACT −

3 - 0 = 3
3 - 1 = 2
3 - 2 = 1
3 - 3 = 0

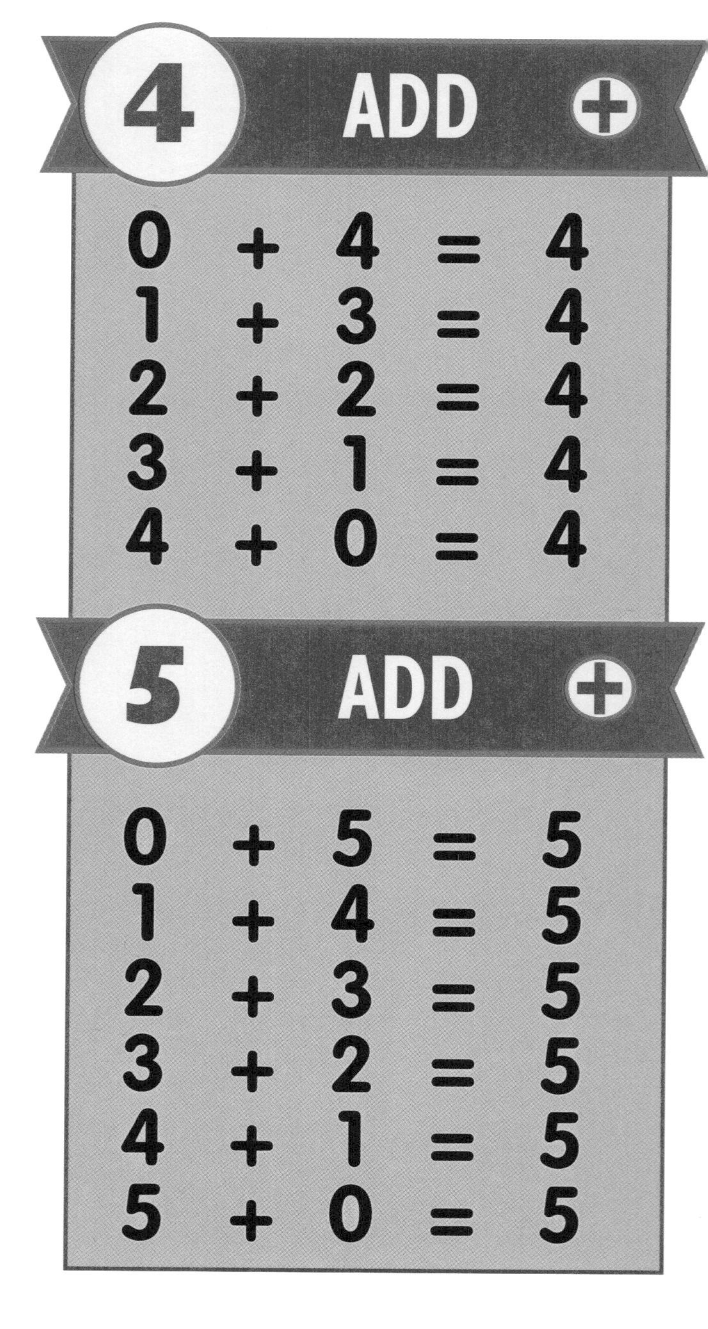

4 ADD +
0 + 4 = 4
1 + 3 = 4
2 + 2 = 4
3 + 1 = 4
4 + 0 = 4
5 ADD +
0 + 5 = 5
1 + 4 = 5
2 + 3 = 5
3 + 2 = 5
4 + 1 = 5
5 + 0 = 5

## 4 SUBTRACT −

4 - 0 = 4
4 - 1 = 3
4 - 2 = 2
4 - 3 = 1
4 - 4 = 0

## 5 SUBTRACT −

5 - 0 = 5
5 - 1 = 4
5 - 2 = 3
5 - 3 = 2
5 - 4 = 1
5 - 5 = 0

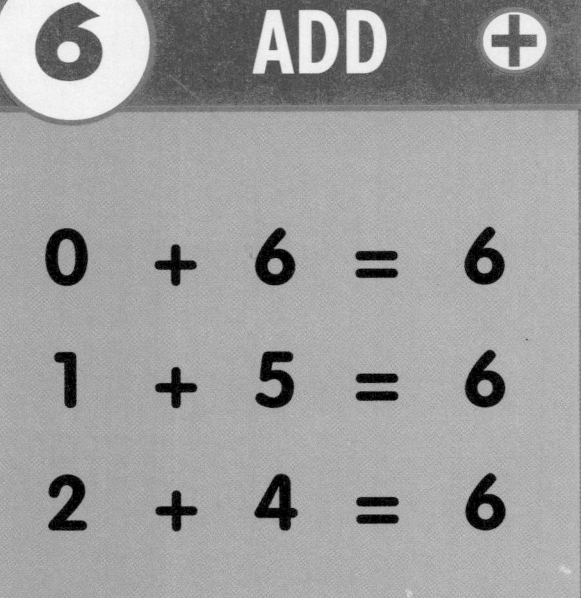


$0 + 6 = 6$

$1 + 5 = 6$

$2 + 4 = 6$

$3 + 3 = 6$

$4 + 2 = 6$

$5 + 1 = 6$

$6 + 0 = 6$

# 6 SUBTRACT −

6 - 6 = 0

6 - 5 = 1

6 - 4 = 2

6 - 3 = 3

6 - 2 = 4

6 - 1 = 5

6 - 0 = 6

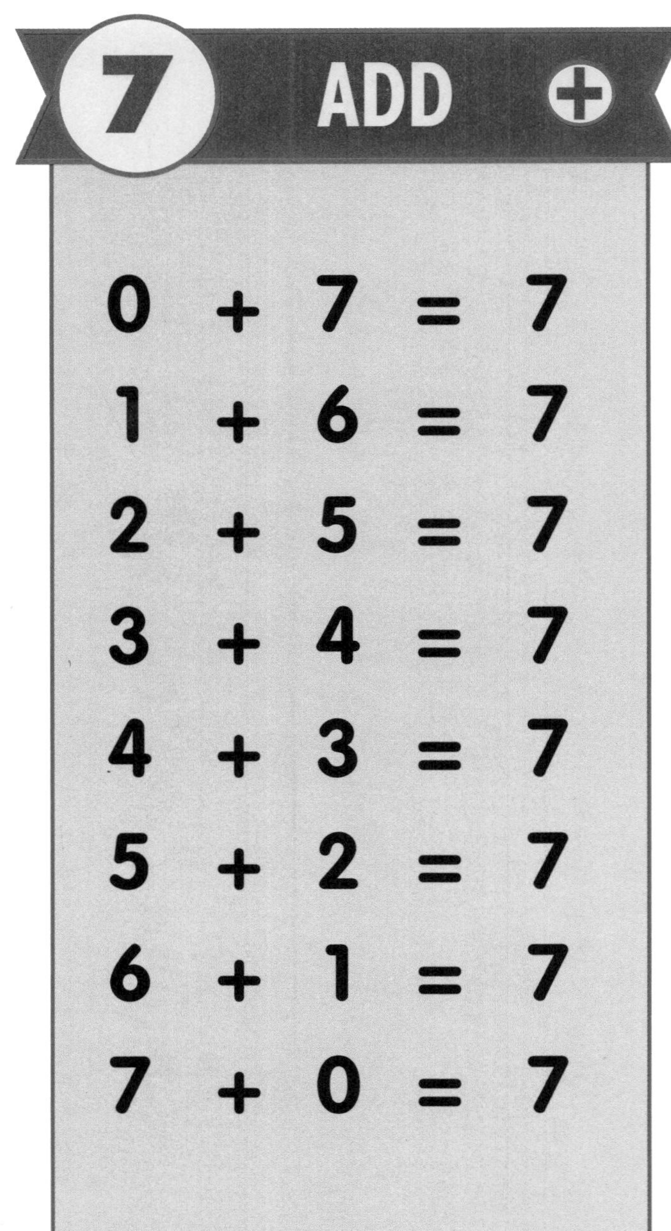
7
ADD
0 + 7 = 7
1 + 6 = 7
2 + 5 = 7
3 + 4 = 7
4 + 3 = 7
5 + 2 = 7
6 + 1 = 7
7 + 0 = 7

# 7 SUBTRACT −

7 - 0 = 7

7 - 1 = 6

7 - 2 = 5

7 - 3 = 4

7 - 4 = 3

7 - 5 = 2

7 - 6 = 1

7 - 7 = 0

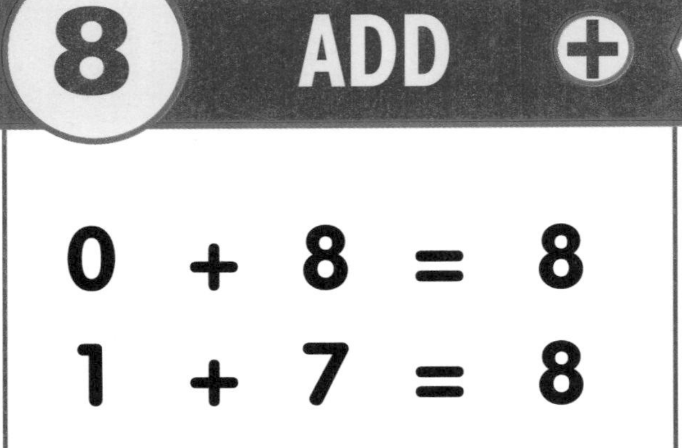

# 8 ADD

$0 + 8 = 8$

$1 + 7 = 8$

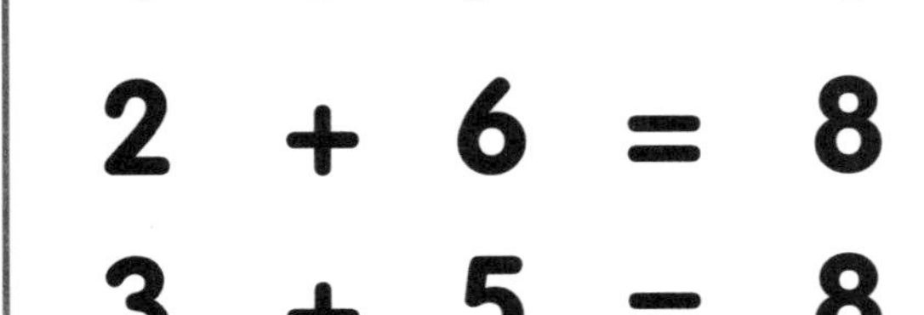

$2 + 6 = 8$

$3 + 5 = 8$

$4 + 4 = 8$

$5 + 3 = 8$

$6 + 2 = 8$

$7 + 1 = 8$

$8 + 0 = 8$

# 8 SUBTRACT −

8 - 0 = 8

8 - 1 = 7

8 - 2 = 6

8 - 3 = 5

8 - 4 = 4

8 - 5 = 3

8 - 6 = 2

8 - 7 = 1

8 - 8 = 0

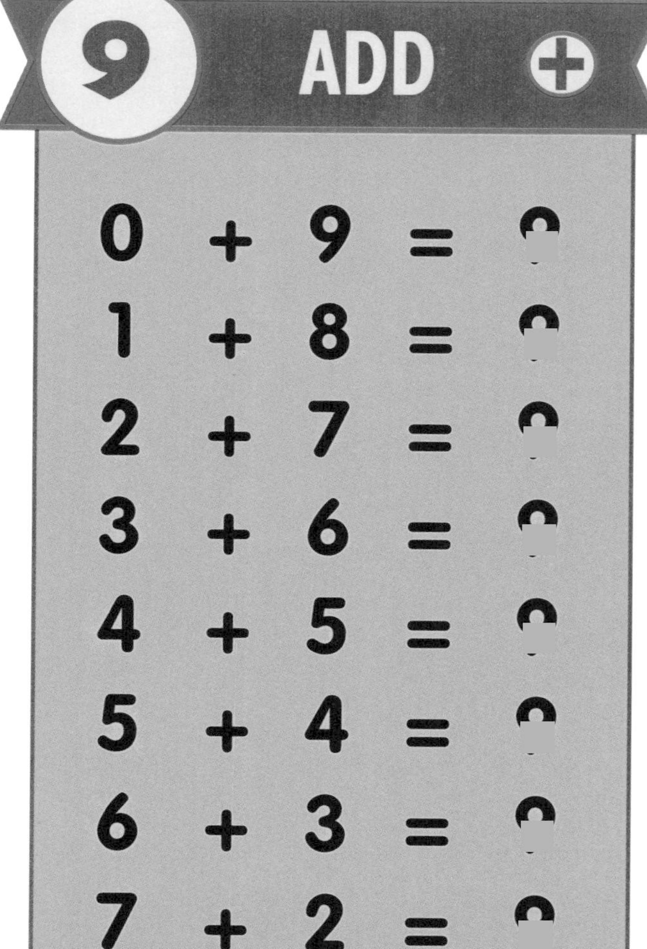


8 + 1 =

9 + 0 = 9

9 - 0 = 9

9 - 1 = 8

9 - 2 = 7

9 - 3 = 6

9 - 4 = 5

9 - 5 = 4

9 - 6 = 3

9 - 7 = 2

9 - 8 = 1

9 - 9 = 0

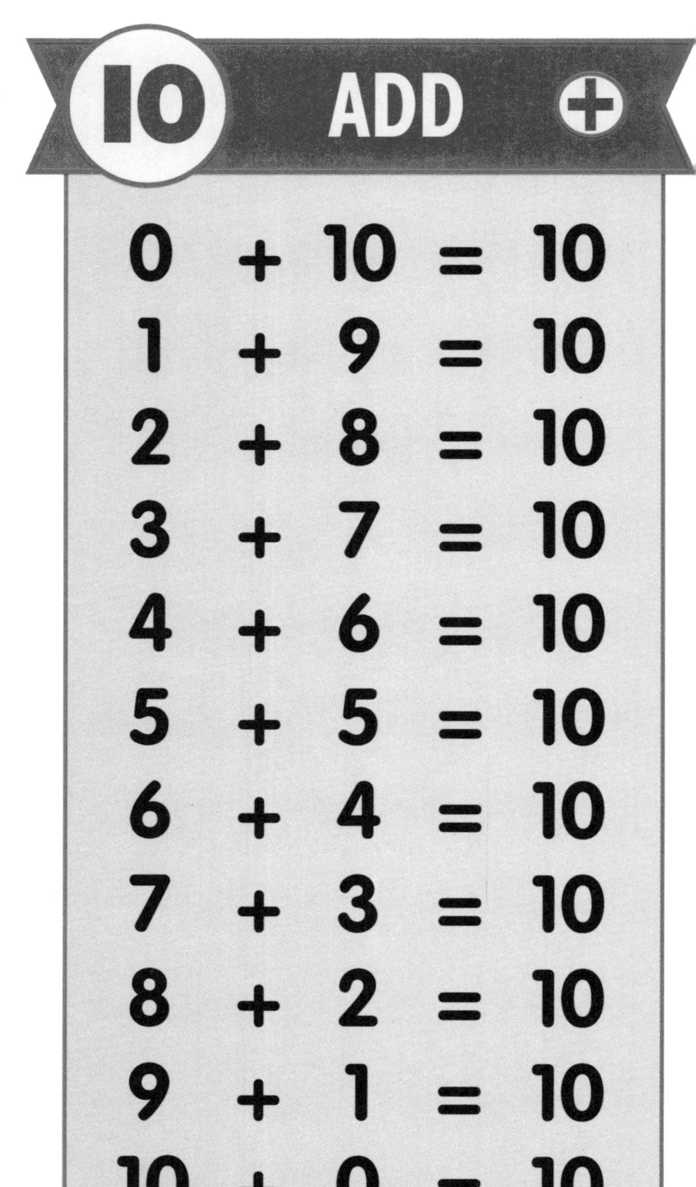
10
ADD
+
0 + 10 = 10
1 + 9 = 10
2 + 8 = 10
3 + 7 = 10
4 + 6 = 10
5 + 5 = 10
6 + 4 = 10
7 + 3 = 10
8 + 2 = 10
9 + 1 = 10
10 + 0 = 10

# 10 SUBTRACT −

10 - 0 = 10
10 - 1 = 9
10 - 2 = 8
10 - 3 = 7
10 - 4 = 6
10 - 5 = 5
10 - 6 = 4
10 - 7 = 3
10 - 8 = 2
10 - 9 = 1
10 - 10 = 0

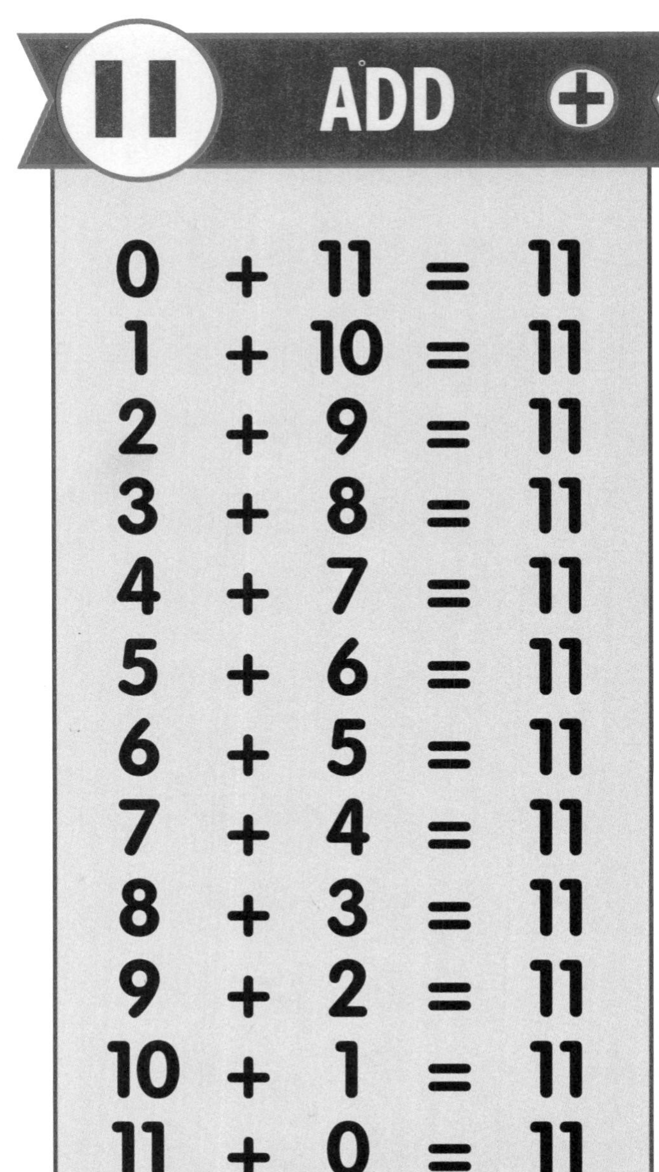
11
ADD
0 + 11 = 11
1 + 10 = 11
2 + 9 = 11
3 + 8 = 11
4 + 7 = 11
5 + 6 = 11
6 + 5 = 11
7 + 4 = 11
8 + 3 = 11
9 + 2 = 11
10 + 1 = 11
11 + 0 = 11

# 11 SUBTRACT −

$11 - 0 = 11$
$11 - 1 = 10$
$11 - 2 = 9$
$11 - 3 = 8$
$11 - 4 = 7$
$11 - 5 = 6$
$11 - 6 = 5$
$11 - 7 = 4$
$11 - 8 = 3$
$11 - 9 = 2$
$11 - 10 = 1$
$11 - 11 = 0$

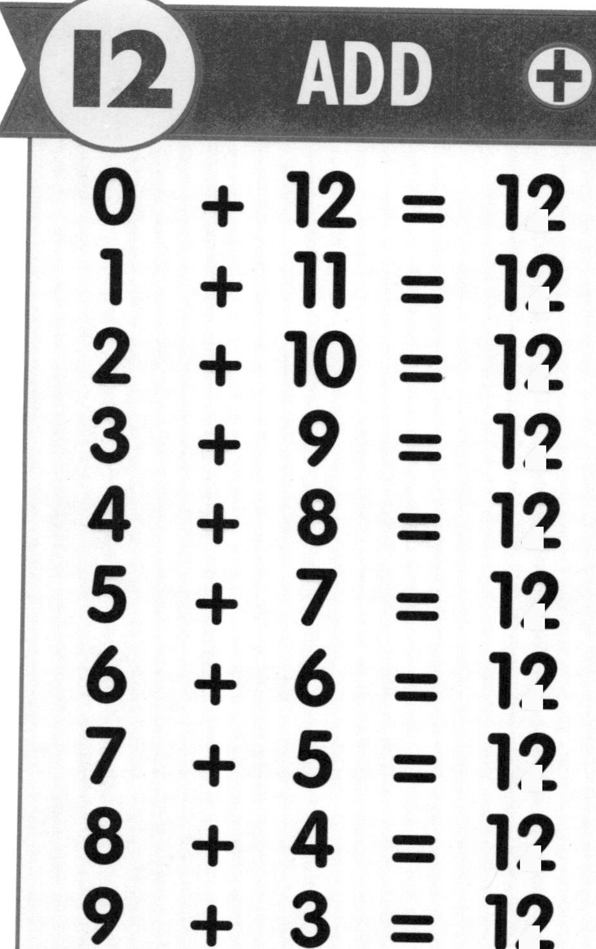

# 12 ADD +

0 + 12 = 12
1 + 11 = 12
2 + 10 = 12
3 + 9 = 12
4 + 8 = 12
5 + 7 = 12
6 + 6 = 12
7 + 5 = 12
8 + 4 = 12
9 + 3 = 12
10 + 2 = 12
11 + 1 = 12
12 + 0 = 12

# 12 SUBTRACT −

12 − 0 = 12
12 − 1 = 11
12 − 2 = 10
12 − 3 = 9
12 − 4 = 8
12 − 5 = 7
12 − 6 = 6
12 − 7 = 5
12 − 8 = 4
12 − 9 = 3
12 − 10 = 2
12 − 11 = 1
12 − 12 = 0

# INSTANT ANSWER

This instant answer number matrix adds and subtracts for you !

Add:
To work out 9 + 4, first find 9 in the number matrix. Then count on 4 squares. Your answer should be 13.
9 + 4 = 13

Subtract:
To work out 45 - 6, first find 45 in the number matrix. Then count back 6 squares. Your answer should be 39.
45 - 6 = 39

> When you come to the end of a line in the matrix, go to the opposite end of the next line and keep counting.

Try using the number matrix to find the answers to these questions:

3 + 7 = ?    5 + 5 = ?    4 + 8 = ?

12 - 3 = ?    10 - 7 = ?    8 - 6 = ?

# NUMBER MATRIX

| | | | | | | | | | |
|---|---|---|---|---|---|---|---|---|---|
| 1 | 2 | 3 | 4 | 5 | 6 | 7 | 8 | 9 | 10 |
| 11 | 12 | 13 | 14 | 15 | 16 | 17 | 18 | 19 | 20 |
| 21 | 22 | 23 | 24 | 25 | 26 | 27 | 28 | 29 | 30 |
| 31 | 32 | 33 | 34 | 35 | 36 | 37 | 38 | 39 | 40 |
| 41 | 42 | 43 | 44 | 45 | 46 | 47 | 48 | 49 | 50 |
| 51 | 52 | 53 | 54 | 55 | 56 | 57 | 58 | 59 | 60 |
| 61 | 62 | 63 | 64 | 65 | 66 | 67 | 68 | 69 | 70 |
| 71 | 72 | 73 | 74 | 75 | 76 | 77 | 78 | 79 | 80 |
| 81 | 82 | 83 | 84 | 85 | 86 | 87 | 88 | 89 | 90 |
| 91 | 92 | 93 | 94 | 95 | 96 | 97 | 98 | 99 | 100 |

**Turn to the next page to test what you have learned.**

# ADD

Test your addition skills :

| | |
|---|---|
| $3 + 4 = ?$ | $2 + 5 = ?$ |
| $5 + 7 = ?$ | $9 + 2 = ?$ |
| $6 + 4 = ?$ | $4 + 4 = ?$ |
| $8 + 2 = ?$ | $5 + 4 = ?$ |
| $10 + 4 = ?$ | $3 + 5 = ?$ |
| $15 + 3 = ?$ | $25 + 5 = ?$ |

Use the number matrix to help you. Check your answers against the tables.

# SUBTRACT

Test your subtraction skills :

| | |
|---|---|
| 10 - 4 = ? | 9 - 5 = ? |
| 7 - 2 = ? | 6 - 4 = ? |
| 12 - 6 = ? | 11 - 6 = ? |
| 6 - 3 = ? | 12 - 4 = ? |
| 12 - 2 = ? | 8 - 5 = ? |
| 14 - 2 = ? | 40 - 10 = ? |

Use the number matrix to help you. Check your answers against the tables.

First published 2000 by Armadillo Books
An imprint of Bookmart Limited
Desford Road, Enderby
Leicester LE9 5AD
England



ISBN 1-90046-647-3

Printed in Spain